# Where Animals Live
# Rainforest Animals

By Katie Buckley

2  I see sloths in the rainforest.

I see tree frogs in the rainforest.

I see toucans in the rainforest.

I see jaguars in the rainforest.

I see geckos in the rainforest.

I see monkeys in the rainforest.

I see snakes in the rainforest.

I see chameleons in the rainforest.

10 I see macaws in the rainforest.

I see lemurs in the rainforest.

I see orangutans
in the rainforest.

I see hummingbirds
in the rainforest.

# Word List

## vocabulary words

| | | |
|---|---|---|
| rainforest | jaguars | macaws |
| sloths | geckos | lemurs |
| tree | monkeys | orangutans |
| frogs | snakes | hummingbirds |
| toucans | chameleons | |

# 73 Words

I see sloths in the rainforest.

I see tree frogs in the rainforest.

I see toucans in the rainforest.

I see jaguars in the rainforest.

I see geckos in the rainforest.

I see monkeys in the rainforest.

I see snakes in the rainforest.

I see chameleons in the rainforest.

I see macaws in the rainforest.

I see lemurs in the rainforest.

I see orangutans in the rainforest.

I see hummingbirds in the rainforest.

Published in the United States of America by Cherry Lake Publishing Group
Ann Arbor, Michigan
www.cherrylakepublishing.com

Photo Credits: © Travel Stock/Shutterstock, cover; © Kurit afshen/Shutterstock, title page; © Lukas Kovarik/Shutterstock, 2; © Ondrej Prosicky/Shutterstock, 3; © crbellette/Shutterstock, 4; © Patryk Kosmider/Shutterstock, 5; © DWI YULIANTO/Shutterstock, 6; © Hung Chung Chih/Shutterstock, 7; © Kurit afshen/Shutterstock, 8; © Gaschwald/Shutterstock, 9; © Martin Mecnarowski/Shutterstock, 10; © Ondrej_Novotny_92/Shutterstock, 11; © Boule/Shutterstock, 12; © Ondrej Prosicky/Shutterstock, 13; © apple2499/Shutterstock, 14

Copyright © 2024 by Cherry Lake Publishing Group
All rights reserved. No part of this book may be reproduced or utilized
in any form or by any means without written permission from the publisher.

Note from publisher: Websites change regularly, and their future contents are outside of our control. Supervise children when conducting any recommended online searches for extended learning opportunities.

**Cherry Blossom Press** is an imprint of Cherry Lake Publishing Group.

Library of Congress Cataloging-in-Publication Data

Names: Buckley, Katie (Children's author), author.
Title: Rainforest animals / written by: Katie Buckley..
Description: Ann Arbor, Michigan : Cherry Blossom Press, 2024. | Series: Where animals live | Audience: Grades K-1 | Summary: "Rainforest Animals showcases animals found in a rainforest environment, including animals like sloths and tree frogs. Uses the Whole Language approach to literacy, combining sight words and repetition. Simple text makes reading these books easy and fun. Bold, colorful photographs that align directly with the text help readers with comprehension"– Provided by publisher.
Identifiers: LCCN 2023035088 | ISBN 9781668937624 (paperback) | ISBN 9781668940006 (ebook) | ISBN 9781668941355 (pdf)
Subjects: LCSH: Rain forest animals–Juvenile literature. | Rain forest ecology–Juvenile literature.
Classification: LCC QL112 .B85 2024 | DDC 591.734–dc23/eng/20230811
LC record available at https://lccn.loc.gov/2023035088

Printed in the United States of America
Corporate Graphics

**Katie Buckley** grew up in Michigan and continues to call the Mitten her home. When she's not writing and editing, you'll find her gardening, playing music, and spending time with her dog, Scout. She has always loved books and animals, so she's a big fan of this series.